Simplifies what, why, how & Possibilities of Metaverse

THE BUSINESS OF METAVERSE

Kireeti Kesavamurthy

The Business of Metaverse

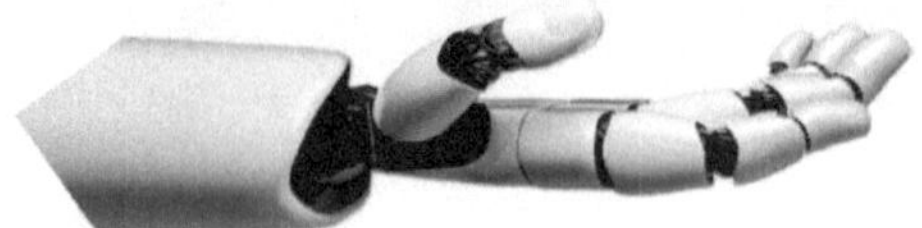

Simplifies what, why, how & possibilities of metaverse

- Kireeti Kesavamurthy

Disclaimer:

The information contained in this book is intended for general information purposes only. While we have made every effort to ensure the accuracy and completeness of the information provided, we make no representations or warranties of any kind, express or implied, about the completeness, accuracy, reliability, suitability, or availability with respect to the information, products, services, or related graphics contained in this book for any purpose.

The use of any information provided in this book is solely at your own risk. We will not be liable for any loss or damage, including without limitation, indirect or consequential loss or damage, or any loss or damage whatsoever arising from loss of data or profits arising out of, or in connection with, the use of this book.

Any reliance you place on the information contained in this book is therefore strictly at your own risk. The inclusion of any links or references to other resources or websites does not necessarily imply a recommendation or endorse the views expressed within them.

Every effort is made to keep this book up and running smoothly. However, we take no responsibility for, and will not be liable for, the book being temporarily unavailable due to technical issues beyond our control.

The content of this book represents the opinions of the author and should not be construed as professional advice. Please consult with a qualified professional before taking any action based on the information provided in this book.

To
SHIVA — The master of universe

CONTENTS & STRUCTURE

INTRODUCTION

We all live in a world where we do different things, perform many actions, work, communicate, go through emotions, play different games, go on recreational outings & adventure trips.

All these happens at different times and at different locations, you may need to take time off from your work, spend money and travel to needed locations to experience these aspects of fun, excitement, adventure and emotions.

Imagine if you can experience similar indulgence in the comfort of your home or office! - The technology that makes it happen is 'Metaverse'.

The Metaverse is like a giant playground or a really big video game or a vast landscape or a city, it can also be a combination of all these. All of these are developed, created and made available virtually. These are accessible through any of the smart devices or laptops. In this playground (virtual place), you get to create your own character, which is called an avatar. You can make your avatar look however you want; you can even change its clothes and accessories - avatars are the digital representations of ourselves.

Here's the coolest part - you get to meet and play with other people's avatars from all over the world! You can talk to them, play games with them, and even do fun activities together in virtual environments. These environments could be anything from fully realized cities and landscapes to fantastical worlds and sci-fi universes!

Experiencing metaverse is like, you are playing a video game, and at the same time you are actually inside it. You can interact with everything and everyone around you. The indulging experience is elevated with virtual reality goggles which make you feel you are actually present in the virtual world doing what you enjoy.

In effect metaverse is a man-made virtual world where you can do anything and everything which it offers from work to adventure activities; from learning to simulations.... and so on.

The Metaverse is a term used to describe a hypothetical place, in which we will be able to interact with digital worlds and virtual reality in a way that feels just as real as the physical world.

The Metaverse is being built on the latest of virtual and augmented reality technologies, which is designed to make these experiences as immersive and realistic as possible. With advances in graphics and processing power, the Metaverse will be able to offer experiences that feel almost indistinguishable from the real world.

One of the most exciting aspects of the Metaverse is the potential for it to become a fully-realized economy, with virtual goods and services being bought and sold using digital currencies. This could lead to a whole new way of working, with people able to earn a living entirely within the Metaverse, creating and selling their own digital products and services.

While the Metaverse is still in its early stages, there is a lot of excitement around the potential it holds in changing the way we interact with each other and with technology. It's an exciting time to be a part of the digital world, and the Metaverse represents the next big leap forward in how we engage with it.

Remember – Metaverse is not just a technology or Virtual place, it's an ecosystem.

Metaverse

A virtual universe where people can interact with each other and with virtual objects using avatars. It can be imagined as an immersive, persistent, and shared three-dimensional space where people communicate, collaborate, play games, work, do business and even live their lives. Think of it like a vast online world (universe) where you can do many things you would normally do in the real world, but in a digital form. It's like a combination of virtual reality and the internet.

The metaverse concept envisions a future where physical and virtual reality is seamlessly integrated, creating a new digital frontier for people. It is a decentralized and interconnected network of virtual spaces, where users can create, share and experience digital content, products, commerce and services.

The Metaverse is evolving it's not yet fully realized, but it is being actively researched and developed by technology companies and researchers in the fields of virtual reality and computer science.

Metaverse platforms are virtual platforms that help developers in creating new virtual experiences by leveraging augmented reality, virtual reality and related technologies. Think of metaverse platforms as the bridges between the real and virtual realms.

Experience few Metaverse platforms:

https://illuvium.io/ 

https://www.voxels.com 

https://axieinfinity.com/ 

https://decentraland.org 

https://www.bloktopia.com 

http://metahero.io/ 

Metaverse - Virtual reality - Augmented reality – Mixed reality

Metaverse and virtual reality (VR) are related concepts, but they are not the same thing.

Virtual reality refers to the use of technology to create a simulated environment that can be experienced through the senses, such as sight and sound. This can include things like VR headsets, which allow users to enter a digital world and interact with it using hand-held controllers. Examples of virtual reality include video games, training simulations, and virtual tours of real-world locations.

Augmented reality (AR) combines computer generated content and real world to provide indulging experience. AR technology is the convergence of physical and virtual content such as images, objects, music, sounds & special effects. Users can experience and interact using smart devices, VR / AR / MR headsets. AR technology uses AI, sensors, GPS & cameras to enable real time tracking and indulgence.

Mixed reality (MR) – a technology which combines VR and AR to a real-world environment. Unlike AR, which simply overlays digital information onto the real world, MR creates a new reality that is a combination of real world and virtual elements. This brings in more realistic interaction between physical and virtual worlds.

Metaverse, on the other hand, is a term used to describe a collective virtual shared space, created by the convergence of nearly every virtual world, augmented reality, mixed reality and the internet. It's a virtual universe where people can do many things with virtual objects & spaces using avatars.

An example of a Metaverse is 'Second Life'*, it's a virtual world where people can create and customize avatars, build virtual homes and buildings, and interact with other users in a variety of ways. Another example is 'VR Chat', which is a social platform that allows users to meet and interact with each other in a variety of virtual environments using VR headsets.

In summary, Virtual reality is a technology that allows users to enter and interact with simulated environments, while Metaverse refers to a collective virtual shared universe where people can experience most of the real-world aspects with virtual objects using avatars. Users can hop-in, hop-out & hop-across virtual worlds to experience different themes of metaverses.

Virtual Reality (VR), Augmented Reality (AR), Mixed Reality (MR) and Artificial Intelligence (AI) are the key components of Metaverse.

*Second Life - Second Life is an online platform that allows people to create avatars and interact with other users and user created content in an online virtual world.

Technology needed to Develop Metaverse

Developing Metaverse applications or content requires several key technologies:

Virtual Reality/Augmented Reality (VR/AR): VR and AR technologies are the foundation of the Metaverse, providing the immersive and interactive experiences that users expect. This includes hardware such as VR and AR headsets, as well as software such as gaming engines and development tools for creating 3D environments / models / landscaping.

Networking and Cloud Computing: The Metaverse is a distributed system, requiring high-performance networking and cloud computing to connect users and devices across the globe. This includes technologies such as 5G, edge computing, and cloud-based platforms for hosting and scaling Metaverse applications.

Artificial Intelligence (AI) and Machine Learning (ML): AI and ML can be used to create intelligent and responsive virtual characters, as well as to analyse user behaviour and data to optimize the Metaverse experience. User behaviour analysis is important to keep them engaged and to drive them to visit frequently.

Blockchain: Blockchain technology makes it possible to provide secure & transparent transactions and data management within the Metaverse. Helps to establish digital ownership of virtual assets and to create decentralized platforms for building and running Metaverse applications.

Natural Language Processing (NLP): In order to interact with the Metaverse, users will need to use natural language to communicate with virtual characters and control their avatars. NLP technology can be used to enable natural language interaction, allowing users to speak or type commands to bring their avatars into action with the virtual environment.

Computer Vision: Computer vision enables users to navigate and interact with the Metaverse in a more natural way, such as by tracking their hand movements or facial expressions or gesture recognition.

Interactive Design: To create compelling and engaging experiences, Metaverse content will need to be designed with interactivity in mind, taking into account the unique properties and limitations of the Metaverse medium. This may include things like game design, user interface design, animation & immersive navigational experience.

Spatial computing: Spatial computing can be used to create more realistic and responsive virtual worlds, it involves the integration of virtual and augmented reality with the real world, through the use of sensors and other technologies, which can understand and respond to the user's environment.

Spatial computing is a process of digitizing content. It includes technologies such as Internet of things (IOT), Virtual environments, 3D visuals, VR, AR and AI. Examples of spatial computing includes games like "Pokemon Go"

Internet of things (IOT):   Technology of collective networks of various devices connected with the ability to communicate between the devices and with other systems. Capture and transfer of information is the key in this process.

Internet of things – its convergence with virtual world enables embedding sensor data on to virtual objects bringing in more realistic simulations and responsive indulgence.

All these technologies are still being actively developed, and the Metaverse is a concept that is still in the early stages of development. The specific technologies needed to build a Metaverse will depend on the specific use case, but these are the key areas that will be needed to develop a Metaverse.

Metaverse platforms

A platform is a set of technologies, tools, and infrastructure that provides a base for the development, deployment, and operation of applications, services, and other digital products. A platform typically includes hardware, software, and network components, as well as APIs and development tools that allow developers to build, test, and deploy digital products. Platforms can be open or closed.

Open Metaverse platforms are virtual environments that allow users to create, share, and access digital content freely, without restrictions. These platforms are built on open-source technology, and users can participate in the development and evolution of the platform through contributions and feedback. They are typically more community-driven and offer more flexibility and customization options for users.

Closed Metaverse platforms, on the other hand, are proprietary and owned by a single company or entity. They have strict rules and regulations governing user behaviour, content creation, and access to the platform. These platforms usually have centralized control and management, and users have limited control over their experience. However, closed metaverse platforms often provide a more stable and consistent user experience, as well as a broader range of commercial offerings and opportunities for monetization.

Both open and closed metaverse platforms have their advantages and disadvantages, and the choice between the two often depends on personal preferences and the specific use case for the metaverse.

Here are some examples of open metaverse platforms:

Decentraland: A decentralized, blockchain-based platform where users can create, publish, and monetize their own 3D content and experiences.

Somnium Space: An open metaverse platform that uses blockchain technology to enable users to buy, sell, and trade virtual real estate.

Cryptovoxels: A blockchain-based virtual world that allows users to create, publish, and monetize their own 3D content and experiences.

OpenSim: An open-source virtual world platform that allows users to create and host their own virtual environments and experiences.

Second Life: An open virtual world platform that enables users to create, publish, and monetize their own 3D content and experiences, including digital products, services, and experiences.

JP Games has developed open metaverse infrastructure for enterprises. It promises to enable collaboration between metaverse platforms. This is an innovative concept to enable interoperability between metaverse platforms.

Here are some examples of closed metaverse platforms:

 Roblox: A proprietary online platform that allows users to create, publish, and monetize their own 3D games and experiences.

 Unity: A closed-source game engine and development platform that enables users to create and publish 2D and 3D games and experiences.

 Unreal Engine: A closed-source game engine and development platform used to create high-quality 3D and 2D games, simulations, and visualizations.

 VRChat: A closed virtual reality social platform that allows users to interact with each other in virtual environments and participate in various activities and events.

 Horizon: A closed metaverse platform developed by Facebook that aims to create a shared virtual space for social interaction and connection.

Metaverse and its applications

Metaverse can be used in a variety of fields, including:

Gaming: Metaverse can be used to create immersive and persistent virtual worlds for gaming, where players can interact with each other and with virtual objects using avatars. Examples of this include massive multiplayer online games (MMOs) like World of Warcraft and Second Life.

https://worldofwarcraft.com/
https://secondlife.com/

Socializing: Metaverse can enable creation of virtual spaces where people can interact & collaborate with each other in a social context. This can include things like virtual parties, virtual clubs, and even virtual cities. Examples of this include VR Chat and Rec Room.
https://recroom.com/

Education and Training: Metaverse can revolutionise education and training through the creation of virtual environments such as virtual classrooms and training simulations. Examples of this include VirtualSpeech and Labster.

https://virtualspeech.com/
https://www.labster.com/

Universities have started offering courses in a metaverse environment.   This is going to change the way education is delivered across locations

Entertainment: Metaverse can be used to create virtual environments for entertainment, such as virtual concerts, virtual movie theatres, and virtual theme parks. Examples of this include VR Cinema and VR Park.

https://www.viverse.com/

Business and Commerce: Commercial Metaverse with virtual environments for business and commerce, such as virtual shopping malls, virtual trade shows, and virtual offices enables trade. Examples of this include VR e-commerce platforms like VPark

https://www.vpark.io/

Healthcare: Medical Metaverse can enable virtual environments for healthcare, such as virtual therapy sessions, virtual surgeries, and virtual medical training. Examples of this include   VirtualRehab

https://www.virtualrehab.co/

Art and Creativity: Metaverse galleria can be used to create virtual environments for art and creativity, such as virtual art galleries, virtual museums, and virtual film sets. Examples of this include https://www.spatial.io/

Real Estate: Spatial Metaverse can be used to create virtual environments for real estate, such as virtual tours of properties, virtual home

design, and virtual open houses. Examples of this include Vpark.
https://www.vpark.io/

Remote work and collaboration: Metaverse is a go to platform for remote work and collaboration, providing a new space for teams to work together, share information, and collaborate in real-time.

Metaverse provides an opportunity for businesses to create new revenue streams, increase customer engagement and enhance greater collaboration.

What is being done currently:

1.   F1 Racing in Metaverse – Lot of innovation and possibilities are being built in this space.

2.   Living in Metaverse: Just roam in the vast 3D Models with inspiring, soothing visuals with mesmerising music. Just wear the VR goggles hop in and explore the virtual landscape all alone or

with someone in there. For instance, world.viverse.com provides this experience.

3.   Courtroom in Metaverse: Columbia is one of the first countries to test legal proceedings in metaverse. Feb 15th 2023 a court case was held in metaverse. The case was that of traffic dispute. Judge and other parties involved were in their respective avatar's.

4.   The World Economic Forum (WEF) held on Jan 2023 in metaverse in parallel with real location. Participants experienced the forum in 3D immersive digital form. They called it 'Global Collaboration Village"

5.   Gaming - Of course, lot many games are enhanced for metaverse.

Leveraging Metaverse

In this section we shall discuss about how metaverse can be leveraged by different industries - manufacturing to information technology products / services.

Irrespective of the industry type and the products we deal with, the common components of value delivery happen to be it's "Supply Chain".   Be in physical product manufacturing or software product development, the basic components of delivery workflow are around the foundations of supply chain management.

The needed raw material, sourcing processes, production methodologies, storage systems and consumer segments could be different depending up on the type of product, but the basic components of supply chain management remain intact.

Now let us focus on how metaverse can play a significant role in "Supply Chain Management".

Supply chain management (SCM):

"Lifeline of any business is its supply chain"

SCM refers to management of the flow and utilization of resources, material, data, money & people to transform them from the stages of procurement till it takes shape into a final marketable product or service.

SCM workflow includes below key activities:

Planning | Sourcing | Inventory | Production | Location | Logistics |

Components of Supply Chain

These basic components of supply chain remain same at the execution level across industries. Raw material / goods and ways of production may differ. For instance, in information technology (IT) industry raw material is data, final product is software or software service. IT industry is information or data centric, where in supply chain looks at availability of right technical people, gathering business requirements (sourcing), development of software products (production) and its dissemination to end users or customers (distribution).

In this entire chain of activities supply chain tasks remain the same but the technology of leveraging it differs. For instance, distribution of software products happens via internet / intranet, data & products are stored in data centres. In case of physical goods like electronics or consumer durables, there is more of warehousing, inventory mechanics and logistics, costs involved are much more needing detailed level of planning & execution. Each type of industry has its own challenges.

Having discussed these basics of supply chain we shall now look at how we can make use of metaverse as a realm to make commerce happen.

We can look at Metaverse from two perspectives, one as technology and secondly as an immersive market place.

Metaverse technology as a tool has the potential to revolutionize supply chain mechanics by providing new ways to visualize, analyse, and optimize supply chain operations.

Effective supply chain needs near real time data distribution to happen across the operations of supply chain. Data here could be that of planning, demand inputs, predictions, inventory levels, logistics in motion or production design. Each of these aspects can be transformed through virtual reality (VR) and augmented reality (AR) to visualize and analyse supply chain in real-time. This would allow supply chain managers to view and interact with complex data in a more intuitive and immersive way, making it easier to identify patterns, trends, and potential bottlenecks.

Collaboration & communication is the key to succeed in any corporate task. Metaverse brings in added advantage in the way we communicate with people across locations. By creating virtual environments for meetings, trainings, and other collaborative activities, supply chain teams can improve flow of thoughts and coordination with suppliers, customers, and other partners, regardless of location.

Isn't it an advantage to mimic in advance to assess the workflow? supply chain having multiple activities it's always an advantage to create digital twin of assets, equipment & resources, this could be used to simulate the performance of equipment, systems & dependencies to allow supply chain teams to test and optimize their operations in a virtual environment before implementing them in the real world. Imagine the entire production line simulation to monitor its efficiency as teams execute all the chain of tasks in the metaverse.

How about virtual marketplaces in the metaverse where trade of goods and services can happen in a virtual environment, this would provide a new way for supply chain teams to connect with suppliers and customers to negotiate prices and terms in a more efficient way. In the real world communication may happen either by phone, emails, Enterprise resource planning (ERP) software or by personal visits. Metaverse brings in a common ground to login and communicate virtually. It saves cost, time and takes the collaboration to a different level.

Finally, blockchain technology can be used to establish secure and transparent supply chain management systems that can be used to track the movement of goods and services and to ensure compliance with contracts. This can help supply chain teams to improve the efficiency and to reduce costs and risks.

In a nutshell, Metaverse technology if utilized properly it can take supply chain processes to the next level by facilitating simulations, virtual connects, workflow visualizations and thereby achieving overall efficiency and optimization in the way supply chain activities are executed.

Now let's take a look at each of the components of supply chain (which are generic across industries) and how metaverse can help.

*What we can call it as **"Industrial Metaverse"** – specific application of metaverse in various aspects across industries.*

Supply chain 'planning':

Planning is a very important task in supply chain management. It helps in streamlining operations, enhances efficiency on how the dynamics of demand and supply is managed. In the context of supply chain planning, metaverse technology can provide businesses with a wide range of benefits, including increased collaboration, improved efficiency, and enhanced customer engagement. By creating 3D representations of their supply chain workflows, companies can gain greater visibility into their supply chain processes, identify and resolve issues more quickly to gain optimization in cost structure.

Leveraging augmented reality for supply chain mapping allows businesses to create realistic representations of their supply chain operations, including suppliers, logistics providers, and production facilities. By visualizing their supply chain in this way, companies can gain greater visibility into their operations, identify bottlenecks and inefficiencies, and take more informed decisions about where to allocate resources. For example, a company that specializes in manufacturing solar panels can create a virtual representation of their supply chain, including suppliers of raw materials, logistics providers and production facilities. This can help the company to identify the most efficient routes for transportation leading to optimised inventory movement providing greater transparency on movement of material across value chain.

How about meet-ups in metaverse? For instance, a company that specializes in retail can create a virtual meeting space where they can connect with their suppliers and logistics providers to discuss inventory levels and delivery schedules. This can help the company to optimize their stock levels and improve their customer service.

Enhancing the skills of man power is extremely important to keep them in touch with technology and latest tools. Virtual reality-based training and simulation adds immense value. This allows companies to train their employees on how to perform different tasks in a virtual environment, which can make the process more efficient and reduce errors. For instance, a company that specializes in logistics can create a virtual warehouse where employees can practice loading and unloading cargo. This can help the company to reduce the training time and increase the accuracy of the process.

As the technology continues to evolve, we can expect to see more and more businesses adopt metaverse technology in their supply chain planning operations.

Sourcing:

Sourcing is an essential element of supply chain management, as it involves identifying and procuring the materials, goods, and services that a business needs to operate. Metaverse technology can play a significant role in sourcing by providing businesses with new and innovative ways to connect with suppliers, evaluate products and services, and negotiate deals.

Metaverse technology enables virtual trade shows and supplier events. This allows businesses to connect with suppliers and evaluate products and services in a virtual environment, which can be more cost-effective and efficient than attending physical events. For example, a company that specializes in manufacturing can create a virtual trade show where suppliers can showcase their products, and the company's procurement team can evaluate and select suppliers from the comfort of their office.

Virtual product demonstrations and evaluations powered by augmented reality allows businesses to test and evaluate products and services in a virtual environment, which can reduce the need for physical product samples and reduce costs. For example, a company that specializes in construction can create a virtual building site where suppliers can demonstrate their products and the company's procurement team can evaluate and test them.

Virtual negotiations and contract signing is another possibility allowing businesses to negotiate deals with suppliers and sign contracts in a virtual environment, which can reduce the need for physical meetings and travel. For example, a company that specializes in technology can create a virtual meeting space where suppliers can present their products and negotiate deals with the company's procurement team.

Inventory management:

The use of metaverse technology in inventory management can provide businesses with a wide range of benefits and opportunities for innovation. By creating virtual representations of their inventory and warehouse, companies can improve the efficiency and accuracy of their inventory management, as well as increase customer engagement and create new revenue streams.

Virtual tours allow customers and partners to explore a company's warehouse and inventory in a virtual environment, without having to physically visit the facility. This can be particularly useful for businesses that operate in remote or hard-to-reach locations, or for companies that want to keep their inventory secure. For example, a company that specializes in luxury goods may only allow authorized partners and customers to visit their warehouse in person, but with a virtual inventory tour they can showcase their inventory to a wider audience in a secure way.

Virtual inventory tracking, allows companies to track and manage their inventory in real-time. This can help businesses to identify and resolve issues with their inventory more quickly, such as stockouts or overstocking, which can lead to more efficient operations and cost savings. For example, a company that sells consumer electronics can create a virtual representation of their warehouse, where they can see the inventory levels and location of each product in real-time. This information can be used to optimize their stock levels and improve their customer service.

Virtual reality-based picking and packing. This allows companies to train their employees on how to pick and pack products in a virtual environment, which can make the process more efficient and reduce errors. For example, a company that specializes in e-commerce can create a virtual warehouse where employees can practice picking and packing products before they start working with the real inventory. This can reduce the training time and increase the accuracy of the process.

Companies in various industries such as luxury goods, car manufacturing, consumer electronics and e-commerce have already started to explore the potential of metaverse technology in inventory management and are reaping the benefits.

Production:

Production is an integral aspect of supply chain management, as it involves the conversion of raw materials, goods, and services into finished products. Metaverse technology can play an important role in production by providing businesses with new and innovative ways to design, test, and manufacture products in a virtual environment.

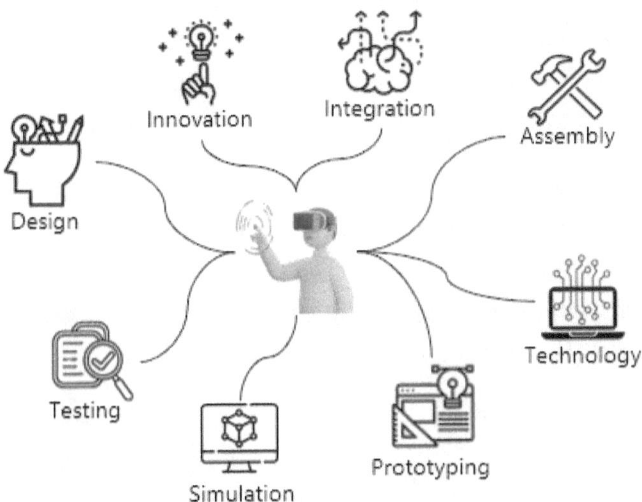

Virtual product design and prototyping, allows businesses to design and test products in a virtual environment, which can reduce the need for physical prototypes and reduce costs. For example, an automotive company can create a virtual design studio where engineers can design and test new car models with different simulations and parameters. Metaverse design studio can be a service as well where in companies can use an instance of the virtual studio for their research and simulations for a reasonable price.

Metaverse Assembly studio for Virtual assembly and simulation, allows businesses to simulate the assembly of their products in a virtual environment, which can improve efficiency and reduce the risk of errors. For example, a company that specializes in electronics can create a virtual 3D assembly line of their factory, where workers can assemble and validate products, which can improve efficiency and reduce the risk of errors.

Metaverse quality studio can help in quality control and inspection. For example, a company that specializes in pharmaceuticals production can create a virtual quality control platform where workers can inspect formulations and its effects based on the knowledge base.

With the evolution of metaverse technologies and its integration with Artificial Intelligence (AI) and Internet of things (IOT) design - production of various products across industries can reach greater heights.

Location & Logistics:

Strategic location is a key aspect in having a significant impact on the efficiency and cost-effectiveness of business operations. Location can be of data centres, warehouses, inventory distribution centres, outlets, technology parks or even the geo spread of infrastructure.

Metaverse technology can be used in location assessment and selection through mixed virtual site visits. This allows businesses to visit and evaluate potential locations in a virtual environment, which can be more cost-effective and efficient than physical site visits. It makes it possible to visit difficult terrains virtually which otherwise may not be possible to get a better perspective of geo location.

For example, a company that specializes in logistics can create a virtual map of its logistics routes, vehicles, warehouses & distribution centres, where in logistics team can monitor them in real-time, assess the movement of goods, fleet management, cargo tracking and evaluate the problems or bottlenecks in the delivery chain. This whole set up could be with augmented reality to either simulate scenarios or to portray the real picture of movement.

Mix of technologies like Artificial Intelligence (AI), Internet of things (IOT), Mixed reality coupled with metaverse can be very effective. These are possibilities and the technology will make it happen. These solutions can be developed in house or it can be a service, say – Metaverse as a service (Discussed in detail later in the book)

Another example, Let's say a 256-kilometre infrastructure corridor project is proposed, terrain goes through plains, villages, private farm lands, hills, historical places and rivers. Few conditions that must be adhered to are, minimum damage to the ecosystem, avoid impact to natural resources (such as trees, water bodies & movement of wild animals), historical monuments & private property. In the present context these kinds of projects are undertaken by doing arial videographic survey of the terrain and accordingly execute the project. The amount of detail that can be captured is limited to videography, but with the combination of 3D models of the landscape, VR – AR - MR, metaverse along with videography mashed up with virtual objects needed for simulation, elevates the perspectives and needed detail for interactive exploration, assessment and execution of the project.

Engagement with stakeholders – Projects where communities, technology companies and government agencies are involved, and need to be consulted & collaborated with, virtual communication with and through the metaverse brings in an added advantage in terms of visual exuberance and perspectives.

The competitive advantage metaverse brings in is empirical.

Case Study – importance of technology strategy and adoption:

One example of an industry case study where the application of technology in supply chain management has had a significant impact on achieving greater revenue is the use of RFID (radio-frequency identification) technology by Walmart.

Walmart, the world's largest retailer, began implementing RFID technology in its supply chain in 2004. RFID tags are small, wireless devices that can be attached to products, pallets, and even shipping containers, and can be read by a RFID reader. By attaching RFID tags to all of its products and shipping containers, Walmart was able to track inventory levels in real-time, which allowed it to better manage its supply chain and reduce out-of-stock situations.

The implementation of RFID technology allowed Walmart to improve its inventory management, which in turn helped it to reduce costs and increase revenue. By reducing out-of-stock situations, Walmart was able to increase sales and improve customer satisfaction.

This case study serves as an example of how technology can be used to improve supply chain management and drive business success.

While RFID technology and metaverse technology are not directly linked. RFID implementation has demonstrated its benefits, similarly metaverse as a tool extends the functionality of the existing tech when integrated with virtual environment. RFID (radio frequency identification), Internet of things (IOT) and metaverse technologies have promising potential in improving supply chain dynamics by extending the virtual environment capabilities for businesses to collaborate, communicate and transact in real-time.

Metaverse — Forces of Supply & Demand:

Supply and demand are two of the most fundamental concepts in economics and they have a direct relationship with each other. The relationship between supply and demand is that the quantity of a good or service that suppliers are willing to offer for sale is directly determined by the quantity of a good or service that consumers are willing to purchase. When the quantity of a good or service that consumers are willing to purchase is greater than the quantity that suppliers are willing to offer for sale, the result is a shortage. Conversely, when the quantity that suppliers are willing to offer for sale is greater than the quantity that consumers are willing to purchase, the result is a surplus. Shortage leads to price raise; Surplus leads to price drop.

Leveraging metaverse technology can help businesses better understand and manage the relationship between supply and demand in order to optimize their operations and improve their bottom line.

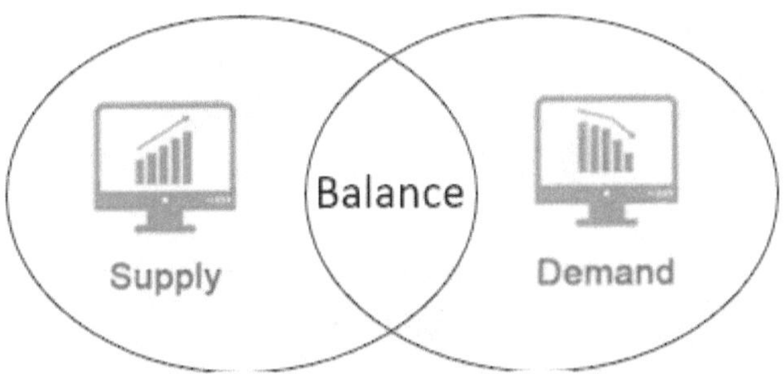

Metaverse technology with Virtual marketplaces allow businesses to create digital representations of their products and services, which can be accessed by customers in a virtual world. This allows businesses to better understand customer behaviour, intent, perception, demand for their products & services, there by the production teams can alter needed characteristics of the offerings and products to match expectations of the customers. For example, a clothing manufacturer can create a virtual marketplace where customers can walk in browse and purchase clothing in a virtual environment. By analysing customer behaviour and purchase data, the manufacturer can better understand demand for different product offerings and make needed changes or enhancements in production.

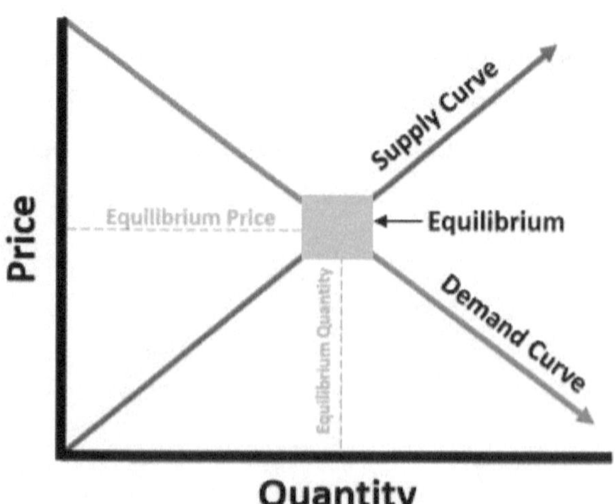

Supply – Demand relationship

This is extremely useful to try new products to analyse and receive feedback before mass production. In the present context companies use certain cities to try new products to analyse customer response.

How about virtual product deep dives & visualization, which can be accessed by customers in a virtual environment. For example, a furniture manufacturer can create a virtual product visualization platform where customers can view and interact with furniture in a virtual environment. They can feel the texture of the wood, experience furniture mechanics and its functionality. In the process customer feedback can be a valuable input to demand planning and product redesign.

Inventory is like a double-edged knife. Too much of it or too less of it brings in challenges. Metaverse technology can be used for virtual inventory management. This allows businesses to manage and monitor inventory levels in a virtual environment, which can help them better understand and manage the relationship between supply and demand. For example, a retail company can create a augmented reality inventory management platform where they can virtually visit warehouses and other inventory locations to track real inventory levels, warehouse space utilization, movement of parts across production lines & movement of people. All this through smart devices, laptops or VR goggles from any location.

Product Demonstrations; Metaverse can be used to create virtual demonstrations of products, allowing customers to see and interact with products in a realistic and immersive way. This can help retailers to increase sales and reduce returns by providing customers with more information about products.

Customer Service; Metaverse can be used to create virtual customer service centres that customers can visit and interact with in a virtual service centre. This can help retailers to improve customer satisfaction and reduce costs associated with maintaining physical customer service centres.

Think about a virtual data visualization setup. Metaverse can be used to create virtual representations of sales data, allowing retailers & suppliers to walk through the corridors of data to visualize and analyse in real-time. This makes data representation immersive and insightful to explore trends, perform what-if analysis, collaborate with partners to take needed strategic decisions to optimize demand and supply dynamics.

In conclusion, metaverse technology as a tool can be leveraged in different ways to make it simple to optimise demand and supply relationships. There by businesses can improve their bottom line and gain a competitive advantage in their respective industries

 An example of a retail company using Metaverse technology is IKEA. They have

created a virtual reality app, which allows users to visualize their furniture in their own homes before they buy it. This can help customers to make more informed buying decisions and reduce returns.

Metaverse and customer relationship management (CRM)

CRM – The practices, strategies, processes and technologies used by companies to manage workflows in relation to customers and potential customers.

Customer is the king – the lifeline of any business. It's extremely important to keep good relationship with customers for long-term success.

Tomorrow's CRM will be leveraging metaverse to provide experiential relationship with customers.

Metaverse technology will change the face of CRM:

Customer Service: Creation of realistic customer service centres with avatars' and needed interactive simulations can elevate customer experience and delight. Saves huge costs associated with maintaining physical service centres. Think about metaverse tech companies offering service centres as a service customized with features based on clients' requirements.

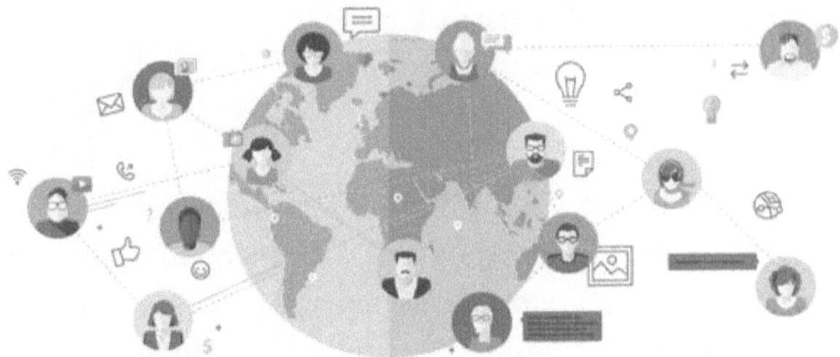

Capabilities could include – promotional campaigns in metaverse, autonomous virtual agents with pretrained contextual & conversational AI to deal with customer queries, virtual training environments with simulated scenarios.

When the world is becoming a global village, it's time to cut the barriers of work places and dive into metaverse to utilize skills of people at global scale. Strategies should evolve adopting technologies to retain customers and enhance their experience.

Tech companies should start providing services to create realistic looking 3D models of offices, cities and technology parks, which can be readily used for metaverse projects – 3D model creation as a service.

Metaverse and fintech industry

Fintech industry is going through a phenomenal transformation in terms of products enabling movement of money across people, entities and places, supporting both traditional and digital currencies. Fintech aims at using technology to improve and automate movement of money.

Convergence of fintech and metaverse as technology opens up new avenues for commerce and exciting opportunity to innovate.

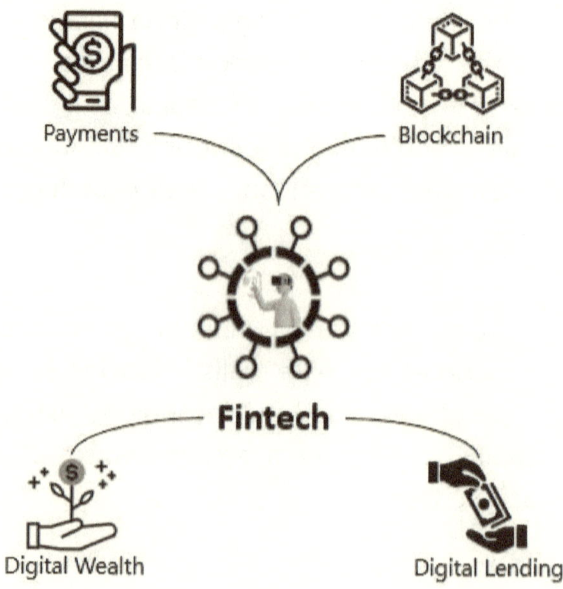

In the digital world we do not feel money, gone are the days where we handle bulk of currency notes for transactions.

How about enabling similar experience in the virtual world for all the transactions that happens in and through Metaverse? Making it fun to simulate avatar's carrying bags of money for gaming, commerce or let's say virtual deposits.

How about banking entities and wallets in metaverse – to handle transactions between avatar's and with real world?

How about Avatar's representing real people in virtual trading of instruments such as bonds, stocks and commodities?

Creation of virtual stock exchanges (representing real world stock exchanges) which any one can gain access to experience and trade in stocks. Except for the members of the exchanges, none of us have experienced trading on the floor of the stock exchanges, we can bring that experience in metaverse.

Think about a realistic 3D model of Bombay Stock Exchange in the metaverse which investors can enter from New York and indulging in trading experience.

Technology has the potential to revolutionize the fintech industry by providing new ways to visualize, analyse, and optimize financial operations.

When we look at fintech & metaverse together, opportunities in creating new products are massive.

Needed technologies are at our disposal, it's the matter of tech giants integrating and extending it to different use cases. Potential of revenue generation is huge. We need to wait and watch for the tech to mature and become less expensive in cost and in creation of content for metaverse.

Artificial Intelligence (AI), Internet of things (IOT), High-definition 3D modelling, Blockchain, Internet bandwidth, Infrastructure platforms and People, together can create indulging metaverse arena.

Metaverse – Automobile industry

Metaverse provides new avenues of product innovation and revenue streams for vehicle manufacturers.

Vehicles for virtual world unleashes creativity of vehicle designers. What could not be produced in real world could be NFT's in the metaverse.

NFT – Non-Fungible Token – A digital asset that is unique and stored in blockchain. NFT's can be anything digital and unique such as, artwork, music, videos and other creative works. Ownership of NFT's are recorded in blockchain. NFT's are now widely popular with many producing them. An extended opportunity for all artists, creators and inventors to monetize.

Let us take a look at how Metaverse technology adds immense value to the supply chain of vehicle manufacturing process in several ways:

Prototyping: Creating a working prototype of a physical model is an expensive process. With the integration of technologies such as 3D Virtual terrain design, Virtual CAD, IOT devices, AI, VR and metaverse, possibilities of creating working proto types and its performance testing under different circumstances can be scientifically simulated. Virtual prototyping enables even 3D driving simulation in metaverse   with   vehicle   performance   being monitored. This process not only provides all the needed statistics to decide on physical car manufacturing, but also to create virtual performing NFT's of various vehicles with different configurations. These products provide greater opportunities for value creation.

Training: Metaverse technology offers simulated multi-terrain virtual environment for training programs for factory workers, mechanics, technicians and for customers allowing them to learn and practice new skills in a realistic and immersive environment.

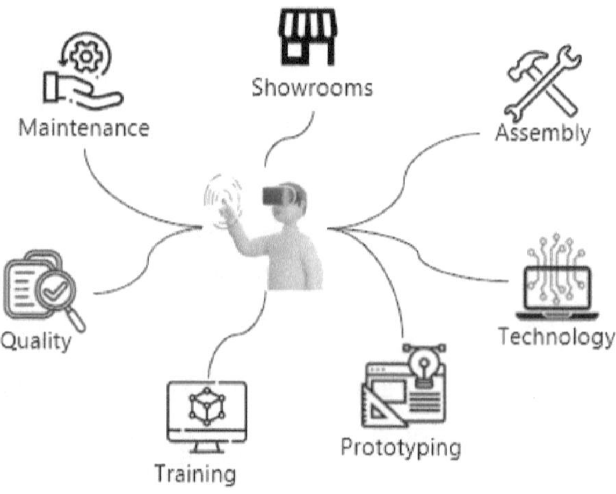

Assembly: Vehicle manufacturing is a complex process involving many components, touch points, dependencies and a lengthy production line. Creation of virtual factory simulating a real-world manufacturing unit with needed components and environments allows factory workers to assemble vehicles in a virtual environment, providing much needed space for production trials, experimentation and to learn. This can help vehicle manufacturers to reduce costs and risks associated with traditional assembly methods.

Showrooms: Corporate giants have already started setting up their real estate in metaverse to showcase products and demonstrations. These facilities enable customers to view and experience products and its features. For corporates it's a space to showcase their NFT and to promote sales.

Quality Control: Metaverse simulation of vehicle parameters, configurations, performance in various terrains provides needed statistics in real-time to analyse and take quality control measures. Which can then me implemented in real world production of vehicles.

Virtual Maintenance: Metaverse can be used to create virtual representations of maintenance and repair procedures, allowing mechanics and technicians to visualize and perform maintenance and repair tasks in a virtual environment.

An example of a vehicle manufacturer using Metaverse technology is BMW, they have created a virtual reality platform that allows users to configure and customize their vehicles in a virtual environment, this helps customers to make more informed buying decisions and reduce returns. SKODAVERSE – Skoda's metaverse.

Every technology brings its own advantages, Metaverse offers a new parallel virtual world which can be leveraged with limit less opportunities for NFT as well as for optimising real world manufacturing. Major corporate giants can even lease out their metaverse environments for other small player to leverage the capabilities.

Corporate Metaverse:

Metaverse for a corporate entity can offer a range of benefits, improved collaboration, communication, productivity as well as increased engagement with stakeholders & partners. A corporate metaverse can be designed to reflect the company's branding and culture as per specific needs of the organization.

Essential features of a corporate metaverse may include:

Office Spaces: Office space where employees can interact with each other in real-time. These virtual offices can be designed to mimic the physical office environment, ambience, including office cabins, conference rooms, and common areas, tools such as whiteboards, screensharing, and video conferencing to facilitate collaboration and communication. 3D models of different office / branches can be created to provide colocation experience to employees across geolocations.

Product Demonstrations: A corporate metaverse can be used to showcase products and services in a virtual environment. This can include virtual showrooms, virtual product demonstrations, innovation centres, and interactive product catalogues / libraries. Virtual demonstrations can be an effective way to engage employees, customers and partners, particularly in industries such as Information technology, architecture, construction, and manufacturing.

Training: Training and professional development can be made interesting and experiential with virtual sessions. This can include virtual classrooms, workshops, and seminars, as well as online training modules and certifications. Virtual training can be a cost-effective and flexible way to provide professional development opportunities, particularly for remote employees. Domain specific content as per the needs of the company can be created and presented in a 3D virtual landscape with impressive graphics and music. Think of it as visiting different virtual portals (dedicated for content) to experience content.

For instance, in fintech domain topics could be on:

B2B payments | Cross border payments | NFT Trading | UPI payments | Digital Currency |

Visualise each of these topics as portals in the metaverse which the avatar experiences in the grand walk way of 3D virtual financial highway.

Events: Organising events such as conferences, trade shows, and product launches for employees, customers, partners, and other stakeholders from around the world with a theme suitable to the occasion, company's branding and culture can be beneficial and cost effective.

Customer Service: Customer support and service is very important for customer satisfaction, virtual chatbots, virtual customer service agents, and self-service portals can be a convenient and efficient way to delight customers, particularly in industries such as e-commerce and technology.

A localized metaverse for a corporate entity can offer a range of advantages, it's up to the creativity of the corporate teams to leverage its benefits.

Metaverse Business models

Plan of action changes with landscape, one approach is not suitable for all circumstances. Business plan for metaverse needs a change in how businesses operate and offer products, services, and experiences.

Metaverse provides an opportunity to offer "New Product Mix" New product dimensions needs new strategy.

To design a Metaverse Business Model, one should consider the following:

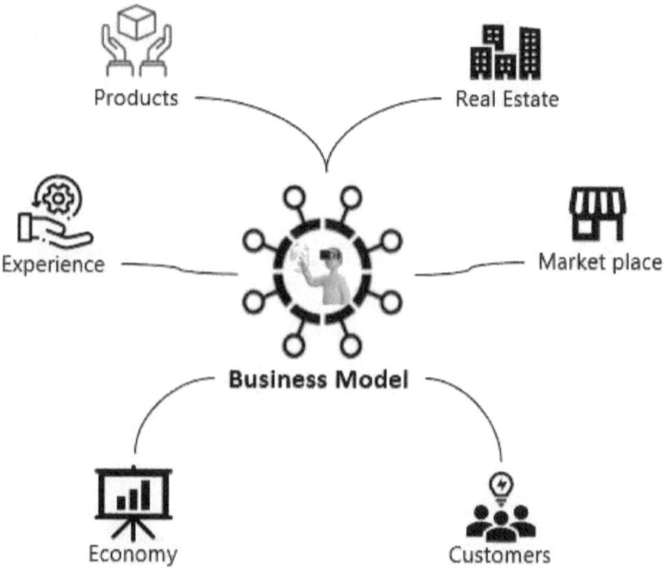

Market place – Dynamics of a market should influence how a plan is structured. Understanding of the Metaverse, its ecosystem, technology, customer preferences and associated operating challenges are essential to chart the plan of action. "Never try to boil the ocean", content is the product in metaverse.

Customer Segmentation: The Metaverse offers a diverse customer base, and it's crucial to segment this audience to understand their preferences and needs. This will help in developing targeted products and services that cater to specific segments.

Real Estate: In the Metaverse, virtual real estate can be bought, sold, or leased. A Metaverse Business Model can include buying or leasing virtual land to build virtual experiences or virtual storefronts to sell products. Supply chain involved in these operations need special attention.

Experiences: Virtual experience that is created in the Metaverse should be experiential, immersive and interactive. These experiences can and should differ from games, events, education, commerce, and entertainment. Visual experience should be engaging & appealing to retain user interests.

Products and Services: Positioning of products & services in metaverse can be looked at from two different perspectives:

First, metaverse as a marketplace for commerce. Products can be avatars, virtual clothing, virtual items, and virtual real estate. Services can be of virtual event management, virtual marketing, and virtual content creation. Real world products and services can also be sold in virtual marketplace. It's one of the medium to promote anything and everything.

Secondly, Metaverse as a tool provides with limitless capabilities to design pragmatic landscape to facilitate business. Creativity is the need of the times. Corporate entities could specialize in offering such services and operational capabilities making use of available technologies.

Economy: Metaverse has its virtual economy, where virtual / digital currencies are used to buy and sell products and services. A Metaverse Business Model should include the creation, management and exchange of virtual currencies and the provision of virtual financial services.

Metaverse offers a unique and diverse platform for businesses to reach a global audience, providing products, services, and experiences that are different from what it has been earlier (real world).

Metaverse and the needed ecosystem has just started to become a focus, as it grows in terms of scale, context and users, business model will evolve accordingly.

Strategies for COMMERCE in & through Metaverse

Commerce is an essential aspect for materialistic existence. Be it an individual, company, industry – one of their fundamental focus is to "make money". Money fuels materialistic growth and ambitions.

Selling in the Metaverse requires a different approach compared to traditional commerce. Commerce here could be that of virtual or real assets / products / services. Virtual assets can be of NFT's and digital content.

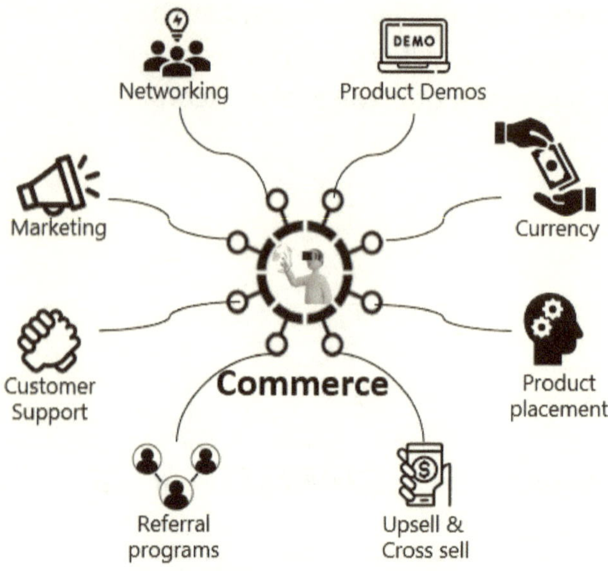

Some of the strategies businesses can use to enable commerce in the Metaverse:

Product Demonstrations: Appealing demonstration of products in a virtual environment, providing customers with a captivating and interactive experience to try out all the features of the product. This can help to build trust and increase the likelihood of sales.

Networking: Networking is an essential aspect of sales, and the Metaverse provides an opportunity to network with potential customers and partners in a virtual environment. Businesses can participate in virtual events, trade shows, and conferences to connect with potential customers.

Marketing: Virtual marketing can be used to reach a target audience in the Metaverse. This can include virtual advertising, email marketing, and influencer marketing. The aim is to create awareness and drive interest in the products and services offered.

Customer Support: Providing virtual customer support can help to build trust and increase customer satisfaction. This can include virtual chatbots, virtual customer service representatives, and virtual FAQs.

Referral Programs: Referral programs can be an effective way to increase sales in the Metaverse. Businesses can offer incentives to customers who refer their friends and family to their virtual storefront.

Upsells and Cross-sells: The Metaverse offers an opportunity to upsell and cross-sell products and services to customers. This can be done through virtual product recommendations, virtual bundles, and virtual packages.

Product Placements: Virtual product placements can be used to promote products and services in a virtual environment. This can include virtual billboards, virtual events, and virtual product displays.

Currency: The Metaverse has its virtual / digital economy, where virtual currencies are used to buy and sell products and services. Businesses can accept virtual / digital currencies as a payment method and offer virtual currency rewards and incentives to customers.

All of the above can be as mesmerising as possible depending on 3D realistic virtual realism created in metaverse to enthral the customers.

How do we monetize with metaverse?

1.   *3D virtual landscaping –*

      Specialised offering - creating 3D content as per client requirements.

2.   *Avatar services –*

      Specialised in creating customized avatars, costumes and allied properties.

3.   *Virtual Shops creation –*

      Specialised outlets in metaverse, a complete package of creation and set up of shop space with product display.

4.   *Virtual Content creation –*

      Content for various topics – training, visualization, music & visual effects;

5.   *Real estate –*

      Sale of space, land in metaverse

6.   *Metaverse monitoring –*

Service to monitor users / avatar activities and behaviour in metaverse.

7.   *Infrastructure as a service for metaverse –*

Services could include, technical consulting, hardware, hosting, cloud space & environments for development and validation.

8.   *Game development –* many players are already in this space.

9.   *Collaboration* services – Google meet, face time & Zoom extending their communication capabilities to metaverse.

10. *Social platform on metaverse –* something Facebook should be working on to take the millions of users to metaverse. Success of this depends a lot on the growth of entire industry ecosystem of metaverse, one company cannot make this happen.

11. *Organising events* such as weddings and parties, with specially curated ambience, visuals, music, characters and effects.

Governance – Metaverse

The governance model for the Metaverse refers to a framework / system of rules / protocols / regulations, and decision-making processes that govern the behaviour & conduct of individuals (Avatars') and organizations within the virtual world. In a decentralized and distributed virtual world, it is important to establish a governance model that balances the rights and interests of different stakeholders, entities, avatar's & communities.

Metaverse is a parallel representation of real world, where in many universes (virtual worlds) exists for different purposes. People moving in as avatars in virtual world may do many things as in real-world.

Metaverse should operate in a fair, transparent, and responsible manner without compromising on ethics, integrity, social decorum and cyber laws.

As metaverse expands breaking the barriers of reach and space in virtual realm, it becomes even more difficult to monitor, regulate and keep tab on various activities in metaverse.

One of the best ways is to adopt, decentralized governance by setting legal & regulatory guidelines to the corporate entities involved in metaverse provisioning & operations. Entities who are the enablers of metaverse by any means be it having virtual business, gaming, collaborators, content enablers & other tools supporting / enabling metaverse in any way should be made responsible and accountable for any happenings in metaverse which violates the set regulations.

These metaverse enablers or parties to the metaverse should come up with virtual monitors & bots to observe and track avatars & gadgets of any kind in the virtual world and take needed action as required based on set policies and guidelines.

With the technical evolution and limitless creativity anything can be staged in virtual world, avatar's may deal with different situations of fun, experience, excitement, threats, unfair treatment, bullying, harassment and so on. To deal with all these, it is imperative that we come up with needed cyber laws for metaverse.

Is it worth investing in Metaverse?

Metaverse has huge potential, it can offer exceptional immersive & influencing experience across wide spectrum of domains. Technologically it is the next big thing to cross the boundaries of what, how & where.

Many companies have started offering metaverse content in tune with available technological possibilities such as bandwidth, CPU, GPU and so on.

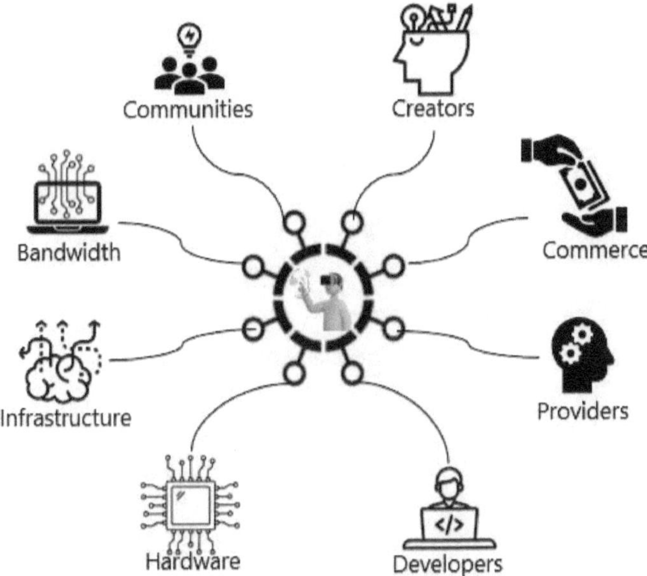

Metaverse market could reach billions of dollars in the next few decades (not years). Many big corporations have started huge investments in this field. Certain estimates talk about $400 - $500 billion in revenue in the next decade. It all depends on economic conduciveness for making significant investments in metaverse ecosystem to make it affordable to develop and to use.

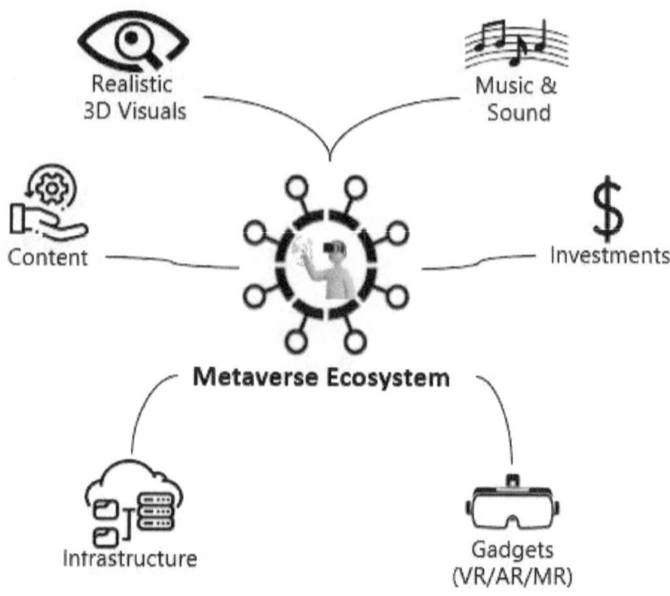

Metaverse is not a product but an ecosystem, for it to succeed, entire ecosystem should evolve in accordance with the requirements of metaverse. Bringing in the needed advancements in ecosystem needs time, energy, collaboration, and money. AR / VR / MR gadgets should evolve and become more affordable and safer, internet bandwidth should go to the next level to render virtual content seamlessly, virtual content generation and delivery should become easy as shooting / editing a video, cost of infrastructure for metaverse should be offendable for more people to create content and contribute towards technological advancements.

All these factors need to be considered to make sensible investments in a piecemeal. Big bang approach of investment by any company will be catastrophic due to long tenure of return on investment (ROI)

In a way, the pace of metaverse ecosystem evolution takes time to reach the levels of expectations we have in terms of making the virtual universe more realistic and graphically fascinating.

Watch out and take one pragmatic step at a time.

The Future

Metaverse as a technology and tool can be leveraged for various purposes as discussed in the previous sections of the book, the most popular one being the gaming metaverse which is evolving faster, most of the popular games are already in to Virtual reality and are building metaverses. We did not focus more on gaming as this is widely known area where VR / AR & MR are being used. With the evolution of metaverse technology what is more interesting is how they are going to revolutionise few of the key areas of mass interest:

Industrial metaverse -

In previous sections of this book, we discussed in detail how metaverse can be leveraged in industrial set up by creating digital representations of the supply and manufacturing chain of activities.

The industrial metaverse has the potential to transform the way manufacturing and other industrial sectors operate. It can enable real-time collaboration between various stakeholders, from designers and engineers to suppliers and manufacturers, in a secure and efficient manner.

The future is going to be interesting on how business entities will evolve to make use of the available technology which will add more advantages and cost effectiveness.

As the adoption of the industrial metaverse continues to grow, it is likely to become increasingly integrated with other emerging technologies, such as artificial intelligence (AI), the internet of things (IOT), and blockchain. This integration can enable more advanced data analytics and machine learning, resulting in more intelligent and autonomous manufacturing processes.

The industrial metaverse will lead to the development of new business models and revenue streams.

Exploratory metaverse –

It's a new area of research and innovation. Exploratory metaverse has the potential to transform the way experimentation and research is conducted. With the right combination of available technology researchers can create virtual models of ideas, theories and hypothesis. It's a cost-effective process where various permutations and combinations can be tried before arriving at a conclusion.

Billions of dollars are spent on research and experiments in physical world, digitization of these activities can save huge costs with the right approach. Strategy around "technology usage" is going to play an important role in deciding who will succeed. Good instance is of how a startup leveraged AI to came up with Chat GPT to put tech giants like google and meta in a fix to relook at their areas of strategic importance.

Ideas   +   Theories   +   Hypothesis   +   Technology

⬇

METAVERSE STRATEGY

It's not the size of the company that matters it's the strategy, technical agility and its application.

Persistent metaverse -

The persistent metaverse refers to a virtual world that exists continuously, regardless of whether or not users are present within it. It is a digital space that operates 24/7, enabling users to hop-in and hop-out at any time and from anywhere in the world. The persistent metaverse is a dynamic environment that can allows users to engage in various activities, from socializing, sightseeing, gaming to e-commerce and education.

The Emergence of the Persistent Metaverse - With the advancements in technology and the growth of the internet, the persistent metaverse has become a more feasible concept. It has the potential to offer a wide range of applications and services. Think about 3D virtual planet of pandora (as in Avatar movie) in metaverse. Where in users can log in and explore the wonders of the planet in a flying dragon. Isn't it a mesmerising thing to happen? a relishing experience of entertainment.

We need to wait and watch for the potential miracle to happen!

Metaverse and AI

AI and Metaverse (as a tool, technology & a parallel 'persistent' world) is a lethal combination. It all depends on how the technologies are used responsibly for the betterment of mankind. AI offers models, algorithms and frameworks to train, simulate, experiment, predict, prescribe and to converse. These AI techniques can be applied to almost any aspect in metaverse from real estate to avatars along the value chain.

Avatar as we think of it today:

> *In the metaverse, users can create and control their own digital avatars, which represent them in the virtual space. An avatar can be customized to look like the user, or it can be something completely different, such as an animal, robot, or fantasy creature. Avatars are often used to communicate and interact with other users in the metaverse, and they can perform various actions and movements depending on the user's input.*

Metaverse being a virtual world, avatars' play a significant role, we personify ourselves to incite actions. With AI coming into picture we will see the creation of semi and fully autonomous persistent avatars in metaverse. There could be may versions of a user avatars in different metaverse portals. We will see many avatar bots active in metaverse representing real world citizens to perform various instructed actions either autonomously or per instructions (programmatically). Introduction of Avatar bots populates metaverse making it persistent virtual world.

Imagine avatars infused with ChatGPT or LAMDA or any large language models coupled with the capability of taking actions in the virtual world. This may sound like fiction but it's a possibility and will happen in the near future.   There is going to be a need for greater governance, regulations, stricter cyber laws and monitoring of avatars to infuse controls in metaverse.

Avatar as a service?

We will see specific apps and services to create avatars which are AI infused with customizable intelligence / functionality as needed. Currently we see avatar as a form with desired costumes, looks and properties. In the future - personification of avatars' with AI is a new game of play.

Governance:

Avatars with AI in the metaverse raise unique ethical and legal issues that needs to be addressed. Some potential regulations to govern avatars with AI in the metaverse:

Transparency and accountability: Ensure that avatars with AI are transparent in their actions and behaviour, and that there is accountability for their actions. This could involve requiring that the AI algorithms and decision-making processes used by the avatars are transparent and understandable to users.

Responsibility for actions: Determine who is responsible for the actions of avatars with AI in the metaverse. This could involve assigning liability to the creators, owners, or operators of the avatars.

Discrimination and bias: Prevent discrimination and bias in the actions of avatars with AI in the metaverse. This could involve implementing anti-discrimination laws and regulations, as well as auditing the AI algorithms used by the avatars to detect and eliminate biases.

Data protection and privacy: Ensure the protection of personal data and privacy of users in the metaverse, particularly in regards to avatars with AI. This could involve implementing strong data security measures and giving users control over their data.

Artificial intelligence ethics: Adhere to ethical principles and guidelines for the development and use of AI, such as those established by organizations such as the Commission's High-Level Expert Group on AI and local IT laws.

To bring in realism: NERF (Neural radiance fields – technology is being explored to create realistic imagery using combination of light, shapes, shadow and reflection.

Metaverse as a Service

Evolution of technology needs wider contributions. Community level involvement is needed to make metaverse commercially viable. Companies with money should not only focus on needed VR / AR gadgets for metaverse, but also create a collaborative offering of "Metaverse as a Service".

Developing "metaverse as a service" is a complex undertaking, big corporate tech giants should form a consortium of tech gurus to facilitate opensource contributions towards a common purpose of community driven metaverse.

Several features can be considered to make metaverse a full-fledged service offering across different industries and technologies such as:

Customizable environments: Ability to create and customize your own virtual environments to suit specific needs and objectives. This could include options to customize layout, appearance, features, and functionality of different spaces within the metaverse.

These environments can be for anything such as virtual storefronts for e-commerce businesses, training rooms for education, virtual event spaces for social or entertainment purposes.

To enable users to customize their virtual environments, a metaverse service could provide tools such as drag-and-drop editors, templates, and object libraries that users can use to build their virtual spaces. How about a capability to upload their own 3D models and real-world visuals to add a personal touch to their virtual spaces? Customization with a predefined catalogue of objects such as adding or removing furniture, changing lighting & sound effects, and adjusting environmental factors to create the desired mood or atmosphere.

Offering 3D model catalogue of real world places is a potential possibility.

All these with the ability to control how users interact with their environment, such as controlled access & permissions to enter, modify or share their virtual spaces.

Cross-platform support: Metaverse service should be accessible from different devices and platforms, such as desktops, mobile devices, VR headsets, and Internet of Things (IOT) devices. This will increase its accessibility, adoption and reach for a variety of use cases and audience.

Compatibility is an important aspect to be considered when we talk about cross-platform support. The service should be designed to run on a wide range of platforms, giving users the freedom of choice in choosing the needed interface to access metaverse.

Irrespective of the platforms & interfaces user experience should be consistent. This means that users should be able to navigate and interact with the metaverse in the same way, regardless of the device they are using. This can be achieved using responsive design, which adjusts the layout and functionality of the metaverse to suit the user's screen size and input method.

To provide a seamless cross-platform experience, a metaverse service should prioritize synchronization and data management. This means that a user's progress and data should be automatically synchronized across different devices, allowing them to seamlessly pick up where they left off, regardless of the device they are using.

Collaboration and communication tools: Metaverse as a service should provide needed tools to enable users to communicate and collaborate with each other in real time using text, voice, video chat, whiteboarding & screen sharing to enhance their productivity.

Real-time co-creation - This feature allows users to work together on a single project, such as designing a virtual space in real-time. This can be achieved using shared editing tools, allowing users to make changes to a shared environment and see the changes in real-time.

Data sharing - Capability to share information and data using file sharing, chat tools and video conferencing can facilitate communication and allow users to engage with each other in a natural and intuitive way.

Project management – An integrated capability to streamline all the tasks of metaverse project is a much-needed feature to plan & execute tasks.

By providing these tools, a metaverse service can enhance engagement, productivity, and social connections within the virtual world.

E-commerce and advertising capabilities: Allow businesses to set up shops & advertise within the metaverse – metaverse as a marketplace.

This feature should allow businesses to set up virtual product showcasing, set up their product catalogues, virtual sales personnel (with AI enabled autonomous avatars in the virtual world for the specific job of promoting sale), integration of payment systems and digital / crypto currency.

A complete tool set to run the business in the realm of metaverse.

Advertising capabilities are important for businesses, this can be achieved using in-world advertising, such as virtual billboards or sponsored events, which allow businesses to promote their brand and products to users within the virtual environment.

Metaverse service could also include the ability to track user behaviour and analyse data to prescribe needed actions to enable better business decisions. This can be an added service at extra cost. The ability to integrate with existing e-commerce platforms, such as Shopify or WooCommerce, can also be beneficial for businesses that already have an established online store.

Security and privacy features: Security should be a top priority. Ensure the service includes robust security and privacy features, such as encryption and user authentication.

Security and privacy features are critical components of any metaverse service to ensure users' personal information and virtual assets are protected from theft, fraud, and other types of malicious activities.

Multi-factor authentication (MFA) - MFA involves requiring users to provide multiple forms of identification, such as a password and a verification code sent to their phone before they can access their account. This helps to prevent unauthorized access to user accounts, even if a password is stolen or compromised.

Security audits, vulnerability testing, intrusion detection, monitoring & surveillance are key components of a robust security package.

Consent as a service is much needed in handling user privacy in the virtual world, ability to anonymize user data, such as IP addresses, browsing history, and the ability to delete user data upon request. These services should also have a clear and transparent privacy policy, outlining what data is collected, how it is used, and who it is shared with (virtually and with the real world)

Analytics and reporting tools:

Usage analytics - Provide clients with insights on how their users are engaging with the metaverse. Analytics should concentrate on user activity, repeated users, engagement, retention, trends, and other usage patterns. This will help businesses to optimize their offerings and improve their ROI.

Transaction Analytics – Provide ability to track virtual asset transactions. This might include tracking the number of virtual goods sold, demand & supply dynamics, and the popularity of different types of goods. This information can help businesses on their product offering and pricing strategies to maximize revenue.

Reporting tools – pre-defined or canned reports and dashboards to provide summarized information, KPI's and metrics across key dimensions will be use full along with ability to create custom or adhoc reports as needed by the users.

Information is an asset, various features such as user surveys, behavioural analytics, trends can be offered to optimize and improve businesses in the virtual world.

Integration with existing tools and systems: Enable metaverse service to integrate with other tools and systems that businesses are already using, such as SCM (Supply Chain Management), CRM (Customer Relationship Management), Enterprise Resource Planning (ERP) systems, project management, and e-commerce platforms. This will make it easier for businesses to incorporate metaverse into their existing workflows and processes. Businesses and individuals can leverage their existing technology investments and workflows to interact with the virtual environment.

Some of the integration examples include:

Ability to use existing authentication and identity management systems. This might include Single Sign-On (SSO) capabilities, which allow users to use their existing credentials to access the metaverse service without having to create a new account. SSO can help streamline the onboarding process for users, while also ensuring that security and access controls are maintained.

Ability to import and export data from the virtual environment to external systems. This will help in building data pipelines for data integration with corporate systems for analytics and other business process management systems.

Integration with third-party applications and services. This might include integrations with popular communication tools such as Microsoft Teams, Zoom or Google Meet. These integrations can help businesses and individuals to streamline their workflows and enhance their virtual experiences.

These are just a few features to consider when developing metaverse as a service. The specific features you choose will depend on your target audience, industry, and business goals, but the key is to create a flexible, customizable, and secure platform that meets the needs of a wide range of users.

These features can be made available at a cost depending on the business model used to commercialize metaverse as a service.

Metaverse - Challenges

The Metaverse presents unique challenges when it comes to governing behaviour, as it is a virtual space where physical laws and norms may not apply. People in the Metaverse may be more likely to engage in activities that would be considered illegal in the real world, such as cybercrime, intellectual property theft, and online harassment.

To ensure the safety and stability of the Metaverse, it will be necessary to establish a system of governance that can effectively regulate behaviour. This could involve the creation of virtual laws and regulations, as well as the development of technology and systems to enforce these rules. For example, virtual identities could be tied to real-world identities to reduce anonymity and make it easier to hold individuals accountable for their actions. Additionally, the Metaverse may need to have a system of dispute resolution and a virtual police force to enforce rules and regulations.

It's important to note that the development of the Metaverse will require collaboration between different stakeholders, including governments, technology companies, and the public. The governance of the Metaverse will likely be a complex and evolving process, as the technology and the virtual world it creates continue to evolve. However, by proactively addressing these challenges, it may be possible to create a Metaverse that is both safe and enjoyable for users.

Bringing realism to metaverse is of immense importance to create appealing, enjoyable, engaging and experiential environments which brings million to metaverse.

Visuals + Music + Sounds + Objects + Vastness

⬇

Realism

⬇

Use cases

⬇

Mass appeal

⬇

Ease of use + lesser cost

⬇

Millions of users

Last but not the least, Metaverse needs massive amounts of investments to reap the value it can offer. Return on Investment (ROI) is a cause for concern. There are many small companies focussed on gaming and metaverse. Expanding their gaming offerings to metaverse – slow and steady approach.

As per the sources, Meta platform's Reality Labs lost US$13billion in 2022 as its virtual platform "Horizon Worlds" failed to attract and retain users.

As per Google Trends netizens are gradually losing interest in metaverse a search term. Its popularity decreased by 75% in December 2022 compared to its peak in March 2022.

In all probability it's not the big giants who will make inroads into metaverse more effectively, but small companies. – Wait and watch!

www.ingramcontent.com/pod-product-compliance
Lightning Source LLC
Chambersburg PA
CBHW031321130726
47988CB00007B/2934